Cool Crafts for HIP KIDS

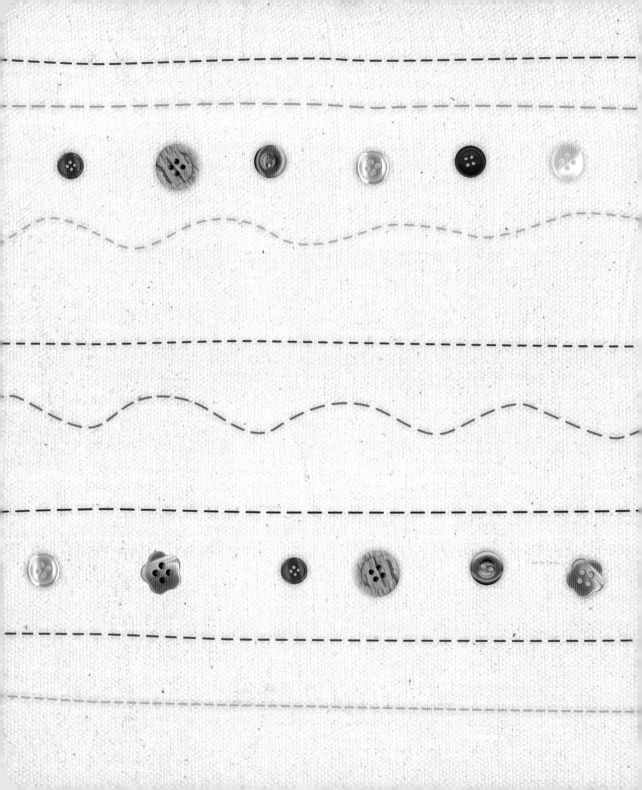

Cool Crafts for HIP KIDS

by Katie Evans

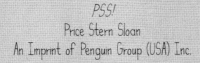

PSS!
Price Stern Sloan
An Imprint of Penguin Group (USA) Inc.

PRICE STERN SLOAN
Published by the Penguin Group
Penguin Group (USA) Inc., 375 Hudson Street, New York, New York 10014, USA
Penguin Group (Canada), 90 Eglinton Avenue East, Suite 700, Toronto, Ontario M4P 2Y3, Canada
(a division of Pearson Penguin Canada Inc.)
Penguin Books Ltd., 80 Strand, London WC2R 0RL, England
Penguin Group Ireland, 25 St. Stephen's Green, Dublin 2, Ireland
(a division of Penguin Books Ltd.)
Penguin Group (Australia), 250 Camberwell Road, Camberwell, Victoria 3124, Australia
(a division of Pearson Australia Group Pty. Ltd.)
Penguin Books India Pvt. Ltd., 11 Community Centre, Panchsheel Park, New Delhi—110 017, India
Penguin Group (NZ), 67 Apollo Drive, Rosedale, Auckland 0632, New Zealand
(a division of Pearson New Zealand Ltd.)
Penguin Books (South Africa) (Pty.) Ltd., 24 Sturdee Avenue,
Rosebank, Johannesburg 2196, South Africa

Penguin Books Ltd., Registered Offices: 80 Strand, London WC2R 0RL, England

Text design by Elissa Webb © Penguin Group (Australia). Internal photography copyright © Tim De Neefe. Page 113: Use of *When You Were Small*
by Sara O'Leary, illustrated by Julie Morstad, courtesy of Simply Read Books.

Text and illustrations copyright © 2011 Katie Evans. Published in Australia in 2011 as *Little Things for Busy Hands* by Penguin Group (Australia).
First published in the United States in 2012 by Price Stern Sloan, a division of Penguin Young Readers Group,
345 Hudson Street, New York, New York 10014. *PSS!* is a registered trademark of Penguin Group (USA) Inc. Manufactured in China.

ISBN 978-0-8431-7062-7   10 9 8 7 6 5 4 3 2 1

ALWAYS LEARNING   **PEARSON**

For Lucie,
with love x

CONTENTS

The Cool Crafts

INTRODUCTION

WELCOME TO THE AMAZING world of craft! Creating beautiful things is something I simply have to do (as did my mother), and happily, my children have also inherited this passion. Crafting stimulates my imagination, keeps me busy sourcing beautiful fabrics and objects, helps me relax while I stitch or assemble, and fills me with a deep sense of satisfaction when I display the finished piece or give it to someone special as a gift from the heart.

Crafting is also something you can do with others, which encourages sharing of ideas and conversation.

And, ultimately, crafting is a creative journey that changes all the time—what you set out to make may not be what you end up with. That is the beauty of this pastime. Crafting can help you develop a flexible mind and good problem-solving skills. The process of making the object will often be just as satisfying as the finished project.

Whether you are a beginner or already an advanced crafter, always remember that no two pieces can ever be the same—that would be boring! And if you find that your object doesn't look like the one in the picture—with a crooked edge or an odd color—consider yourself a true artist because you have added a little something of yourself into every stitch, shape, or brushstroke.

Enjoy!

Katie x

A NOTE TO PARENTS AND CARETAKERS

I HOPE THIS BOOK brings your children many hours of enjoyment as you sit back and watch them create some gorgeous craft all on their own. The projects are designed for children who love to make and do, from as young as six up to any age. They should need little or no assistance, but there may be times when your little crafters need help with something they may find a bit tricky. All materials can be bought from any fabric or craft store.

Start by reading "The Basics" section with them, perhaps trying some of it together, then allow them to continue independently. If your children are just starting out, begin them on some of the simpler projects to build confidence before moving to something a bit more challenging. It's always a good idea to first read through all the instructions for the project you have chosen to make.

Bear in mind that frustration is inevitable, but try to encourage your children to find a way to solve each problem on their own and you will be rewarded tenfold. There is nothing more wonderful than the hush of contentment that falls upon the house while children busy themselves without needing your help. And if you are extremely lucky, you may find that peaceful home adorned with exquisite things they have made . . . for you.

GUIDE TO LEVEL OF SKILL

I have created a guide at the beginning of each project to show you how difficult or easy a task is.

= Simple

= A little bit tricky; some fine motor skills with cutting and pasting required

= May need some crafting experience, such as sewing specific stitches (all described in the following "Stitches" section, so with practice any child can do the craft at this level)

THE BASICS

STITCHES

These projects require a few of the different types of stitches that are used for many kinds of sewing projects, so you will find them very handy to know. It's a good idea to practice the stitch you need on a spare piece of material before you start the project. Ask for some help if you are struggling.

Some points to remember:

- Make sure your thread is knotted at the end before you begin sewing so it doesn't pull through the material.
- Always try to make your stitches about ½ inch from the edge of your fabric (this is called the seam allowance) and each stitch roughly ¼ inch long.
- Always leave at least 2.5 inches of thread at the end of stitching to make a knot.

How to Thread a Needle

There is a little tool you can buy from fabric stores that will help you thread a needle, but with practice, a good eye, and a steady hand, you will find it easy enough without this little gadget.

The needle has two main parts: the point (or tip) and the eye. The point is obviously the sharp end that pushes through the fabric, and the eye is the part you thread.

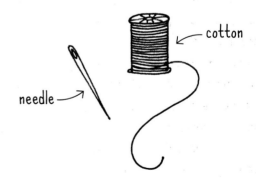

needle ➝

← cotton

Cut at least double the length of thread you need to go around the outer edge of your shape. For larger patterns (such as the Pony Friend), do the sewing in a few sections so your thread isn't too long.

You may also need to double the length before you knot the thread, depending on the thickness of your thread. Cotton is very thin, so a double strand will ensure the thread doesn't slip through the fabric, but embroidery thread is thick, so doubling up is unnecessary. Keep in mind, too, that you will need a bigger needle eye for a thicker thread.

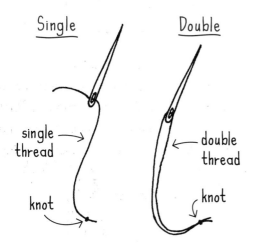

Single

single thread

knot

Double

double thread

knot

Hold the needle in one hand and the end of the thread in the other hand. Wet the end of the thread by popping it in your mouth and drawing it out between lips tightly pressed together. Holding the needle up to the light, push the thread through the eye of the needle far enough for you to grab it on the other side. For a single thread, pull down halfway on the other side, and for a double thread, pull all the way to the bottom of the other side of the thread (see earlier illustration). Then knot the ends. The best way to knot a double thread is to wrap both strands around your forefinger and push the ends through the loop.

← knot

Now you are ready to begin stitching!

Running Stitch

This is a very basic stitch (the easiest of them all) and is used mainly to fasten one piece of fabric to another.

1. Push the needle through the fabric and pull slowly till the thread is taut (pulled through as far as it will go).

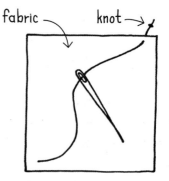

fabric

knot →

2. Leaving a small space, push the needle back through the fabric to the opposite side, then repeat the process, making sure you don't pull the thread so tight that it makes the fabric bunch together.

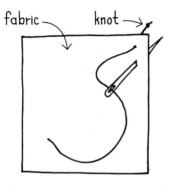

There is no need to keep flipping from one side of your piece of fabric to the other; you can push the needle all the way through. Do whatever feels comfortable.

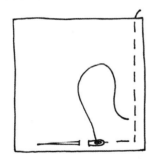

3. Keep going till you get close to the end of the thread length, then knot the end of the thread close to the fabric. And that's a basic running stitch!

Blanket Stitch

Blanket stitch is not only used to fasten two pieces of fabric together, particularly along the edges; it is also a great stitch to keep your fabric from fraying (unraveling along the edge).

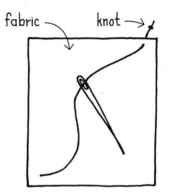

1. Follow step 1 of Running Stitch.
2. Push the needle back through the fabric to the opposite side about ¼ inch from your knot and pull. But this time you stop before the thread is pulled all the way through, forming a little loop.

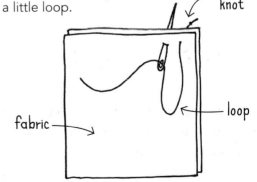

3. Next, put the needle through this little loop and then pull the thread all the way through.

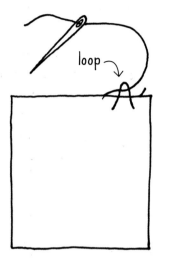

4. Repeat the process, keeping in mind that your next loop will be attached to the first, so it will look a little different.

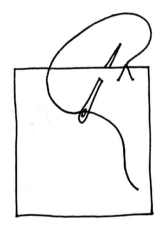

5. Keep going till you near the end of the thread length, then make a knot to secure your stitch. You will see that all your loops have become more like squares running along the cut edge of your fabric.

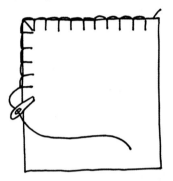

This is a tricky stitch to learn, but it looks good.

Overcast Stitch

Overcast stitch is also great to stop fabric from fraying, and it's a lot simpler than blanket stitch but not quite as fancy looking.

1. Follow step 1 of Running Stitch.

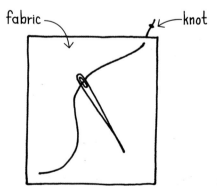

2. Loop the thread over the cut edge of your fabric and push the needle through from the other side, leaving a small space. Pull through till the thread has formed a snug loop at the edge, but not so tight that it pulls the edge of the material down.

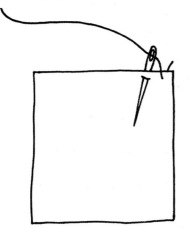

3. Repeat the process till you get near the end of the thread length, then knot.

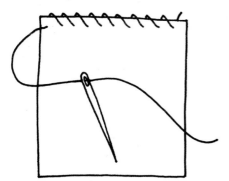

This stitch is one of the easiest!

Back Stitch

This stitch is one of the most secure stitches of all, but like blanket stitch it takes lots of practice to master.

1. Push the needle through the material about one stitch length in from the corner of the fabric and pull till the thread is taut.

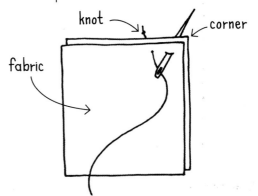

2. Push the needle back toward the corner and through the fabric to the opposite side. Now push the needle back up through the fabric a little ways in front of your knot. Pull through till the thread is taut.

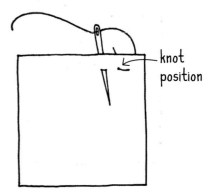

3. Unlike the running stitch, this time you need to push the needle back through the fabric where your knot is (avoiding the knot a little, if you can).

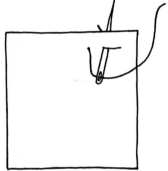

Pull till the thread is taut again, then push the needle through the fabric about ¼ inch from the far side of your first stitch. Pull till the thread is taut, then push the needle through on the other side to line up with the stitch on that side.

4. Repeat the process till you near the end of the thread length, then knot.

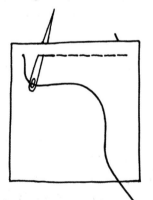

This stitch is quite tricky but fantastic if you want a really good seal on the edges of your fabric. It's particularly good if you want to turn a pattern inside out.

Making a Knot

I find the best way to make a knot to secure your stitch is to sew a little toward the edge of the fabric and, using the overcast stitch, keep sewing over the same area many times, even over your stitch, to create a little lump of thread. Then you can just cut the thread close to this little lump.

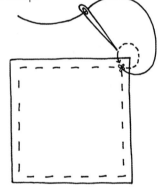

TOP TIPS

* If you find blanket stitch too tricky, overcast stitch will work just as well.
* If you have a lot of trouble with back stitch, try using overcast stitch, pulling the stitches tight. Good luck!

USING GLUE

Glue can be quite messy, so I have a few tips that will make working with this sticky stuff a lot easier. This book uses several different types of glue—fabric glue, glue stick, Elmer's Glue, and strong-binding craft glue.

Fabric Glue

As the name suggests, this is the best type of glue for securing fabric. It usually comes in a bottle with a nozzle at the end and will set clear.

To glue small pieces of fabric together, try squirting out some of the fabric glue onto a plastic or paper plate and applying the glue to the fabric with a Popsicle stick or a paintbrush. This way, you won't accidentally squirt too much glue onto your carefully cut shape. I would use this method of applying glue to any delicately cut piece of fabric.

Glue Stick and Elmer's Glue

These types of glue are the easiest to use and are great for simple paper projects. Both glues are whitish in appearance, but they both set clear. You can sometimes use Elmer's Glue to glue thin fabrics such as cotton onto other surfaces. It might be helpful to squeeze the glue into a small bowl or cup and use a paintbrush to apply it to the fabric.

Craft Glue

This glue is a bit smelly—so you should only use it in very small quantities—but it's not harmful. It is best used on projects that need the glue to be very strong, like the Lace-Pressed Brooch or the Button Rings. Craft glue usually comes in a bottle with a nozzle at the end and sets clear. It's also pretty sticky, so it's easier to use by squeezing a small amount onto a paper or plastic plate, then using a paintbrush or Popsicle stick to apply.

TOP TIPS

* Glue will take longer to dry in cold weather and will set faster in hot, dry weather, so the drying time may sometimes be a bit different from what I've suggested. The best thing to do is test a glued piece by carefully pulling at the edge to make sure it's securely fastened before you use or display your craft project.

* Try not to put too much glue onto your cut pieces of fabric or paper, or the glue may ooze out the sides. If this does happen, don't worry too much—glue used in this book dries clear, so you might not even see it. But if you are worried, grab a tissue and gently wipe off the extra glue.

CUTTING

If you are very careful, you should be able to manage a pair of scissors without too much difficulty. But if you are not sure, always ask a grown-up for help. The projects in this book require two different types of scissors (or shears).

Multipurpose Scissors

It's best not to use the same scissors for fabric as you do for paper, but for the purposes of this book, you should be able to use some fairly good-quality multipurpose scissors. You'll find a wide range in any fabric store— some expensive and some fairly cheap. You won't need expensive scissors, but don't go for the really cheap ones, either—they will probably cut paper okay, but will not be sharp enough for fabric; and they probably won't last!

Pinking Shears

Pinking shears have saw-toothed blades that give a jagged edge to fabric to prevent it from fraying. You will need these shears when leaving the edges of your fabric bare. Pinking shears cut your sewing time in half and simplify some otherwise tricky projects. They are a great tool to have! Again, don't go for the cheapest brand—they need to be sharp enough to cut through fabric.

PATTERNS

The patterns in this book are intended as a guide only. Feel free to enlarge or reduce them— whatever takes your fancy. Try photocopying the pattern and then making a copy from baking or tracing paper. Then you'll be able to use the pattern again and again. And don't worry if your pattern isn't exactly the same as the book's— yours will have a bit of individuality.

LACE-PRESSED BROOCH

Delicate and pretty

meets funky and cool! These gorgeous brooches make the best Mother's Day presents. Try different patterns, shapes, and colors. They look amazing when you wear more than one.

Time

* 20 to 30 minutes to mold brooch and print with lace
* 24 hours for the modeling clay to set
* 20 to 30 minutes to color and varnish
* Total time: About 25 hours— but most of that is waiting!

Level of difficulty

Some gluing required.

You will need

* 1 small pack of white modeling clay (a brand that doesn't need any time in the oven to set hard)
* Some small pieces of lace (This can be bought in small pieces from fabric stores if you can't find anything at home. But please ask before cutting up any lace around the house— it could be your great-grandma's wedding veil!)
* Brooch pins (from most craft stores)
* Craft glue
* Colored pencils
* Clear nail polish

HOW TO MAKE YOUR LACE-PRESSED BROOCH

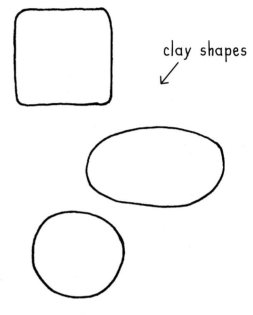

clay shapes

1. Pinch off a small piece from your modeling clay. Roll it into a ball, then mold it into a flat, round, or square shape a little bigger and thicker than a quarter.

shape   lace

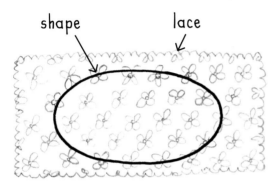

imprint

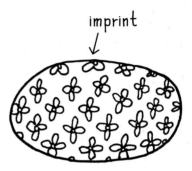

2. Take a piece of lace and gently press it onto the surface of your molded shape. (You could also try pressing the lace on just part of the brooch so you have some flat surface and some imprinted surface.)

3. Carefully lift the lace from your shape. The imprint of the lace should remain in the clay.

4. Place the clay in a warm, dry spot for 24 hours to harden.

nail polish →

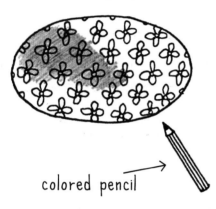

colored pencil →

5. When the clay is hard, lightly color the surface of your brooch with a colored pencil.

6. Using clear nail polish, paint a thick layer over the surface of your brooch to seal and varnish the color. Then let it dry (about 10 minutes).

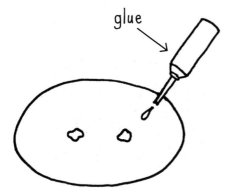

glue

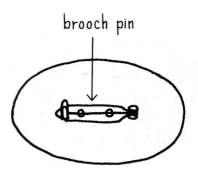

brooch pin

7. Turn your brooch over and carefully place two pea-sized dabs of craft glue to the flat side at the back.

8. Press the brooch pin horizontally onto the glue dabs.

Allow 10 minutes for the glue to dry. (Remember: Drying times for glue can vary in different types of weather. Always test that the glue is completely dry before you try on your brooch.)

NOW YOU CAN HAVE A FUNKY BROOCH FOR EVERY OUTFIT AND EVERY OCCASION.

TOP TIPS

* When coloring your brooch, try leaving the raised areas white and just coloring the indented areas. The contrast looks amazing! You can also experiment with varnishing just the raised areas, too.
* Try pressing a coin or favorite patterned button into your clay. It doesn't have to be lace.

Delicate feathers and intricate webs winding over and into a gossamer bind.

Light as a whisper, a dreamy entwine.

PAPER BEADS

Who would think these beads are made from paper? Make dozens and dozens and thread them into bracelets and long and short necklaces with one or more rows. This craft project is perfect to do on a rainy afternoon with a friend to keep you company.

Time
Unlimited!

Level of difficulty
The rolling is tricky.

You will need
* Some pencils
* Some different colored and patterned paper
* Ruler
* Glue stick or Elmer's Glue
* Scissors
* Ribbon or string

HOW TO MAKE YOUR
PAPER BEADS

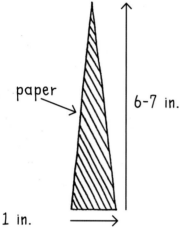

paper

6-7 in.

1 in.

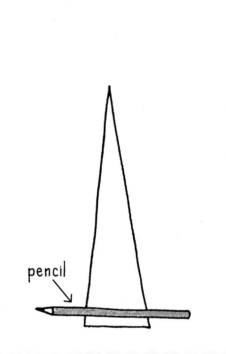

pencil

1. Cut your paper into triangles about 1 inch wide and 6 to 7 inches long. Don't be too fussy about the shape of your triangles—as long as one end is wide and the other pointed, your beads will be fine.

A bit of variety in bead size can be interesting.

2. Take one of your triangles and place it pattern side down with the wider end of the paper closest to you. Then place the pencil across the wide end.

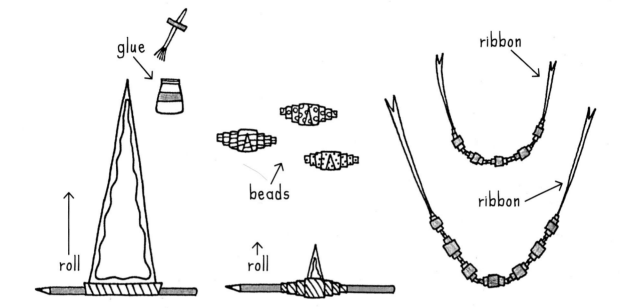

3. a) Roll the thick edge of the paper firmly around the pencil. Hold the pencil in place with one hand and apply the glue along the rest of your triangle with your other hand. Make sure you cover the whole triangle with the glue, including the tip.

b) Roll the pencil forward until the whole triangle is tightly wound around the pencil. Make sure the tip sticks well at the end.

4. Continue rolling your bits of paper along the pencils in this way. Allow about 20 minutes for them to dry. You can make as many beads as you like, using as many pencils as you need.

5. When dry, gently pull the beads off the pencils and thread them onto your ribbon or string.

YOUR NECKLACE IS COMPLETE! WHY NOT TRY THREADING SOME LEFTOVER BEADS ONTO A SHORTER RIBBON TO MAKE A BEAUTIFUL BRACELET TO MATCH!

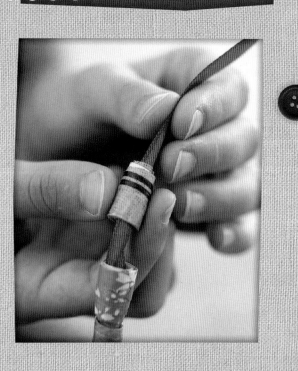

TOP TIPS

* Paint your beads with a coat of clear nail polish before threading them on the ribbon. The polish will make them last longer and give them a glamorous, glossy sheen.
* For a special modern look, choose just two colors for your beads, choose different shades of just one color, or use strips of paper from some old magazines.

Colorful droplets tumbling down.

Strand after strand around and around, perfectly rolled . . .

. . . and beautifully wound.

BUTTON RINGS

Time

About 20 to 30 minutes

Level of difficulty

You will need

* Button covering kit (available from most fabric stores)
* Ring bases (available from most craft and fabric stores)
* Some small pieces of fabric no larger than 2 in. × 2 in.
* Craft glue
* Scissors

Bright and beautiful and so easy to make, these button rings will put a smile on your face!

HOW TO MAKE
YOUR BUTTON RINGS

↑
button

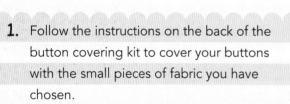

cut

1. Follow the instructions on the back of the button covering kit to cover your buttons with the small pieces of fabric you have chosen.

2. Trim the raised hole on your button backs with some sharp multipurpose scissors (this is a bit tricky, so please ask an adult for help).

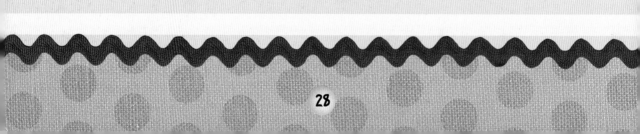

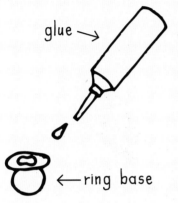

glue →

← ring base

3. Place a dab of glue onto your ring base.

4. Press the flat side of your button onto the ring base that's topped with glue. Allow to dry for about 10 minutes.

TRY ON YOUR NEW RINGS FOR SOME FUNKY FINGERS!

TOP TIPS

* Glue some sequins or little beads to the top of your ring to add some real bling!
* Try to use fabric with a very small pattern. Larger patterns tend to disappear on such a small surface.

Buttons, bobbins, bells, and bows – all things bright and beautiful.

BUNTING

Time
About 3 to 4 hours

Level of difficulty
The sewing can be a bit difficult.

You will need
* ½ yd. of cotton fabric in any pattern you like
* Butcher or tracing paper (to copy your pattern)
* 2 yd. of cotton cord rope about ¼ in. thick
* Needle and cotton thread
* Some clothespins
* Ruler
* Good-quality pinking shears

It's party time!
String some bunting up for a special occasion, or decorate your bedroom to put yourself in the mood to celebrate every day of the week.

HOW TO MAKE YOUR BUNTING

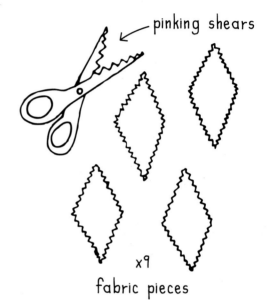

pinking shears

x9
fabric pieces

1. Make a copy of the pattern on page 37. Pin the pattern onto your chosen fabric and cut out about nine diamond shapes using the pinking shears.

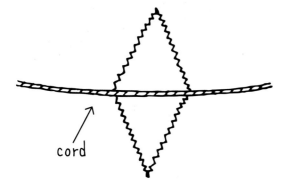

cord

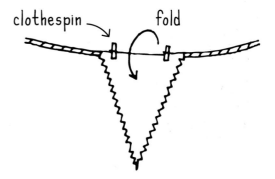

clothespin   fold

2. Take your cotton cord and stretch it out along the floor or a long table. Place one diamond underneath the cord at the center, as shown.

3. Fold the diamond over and clip the top.

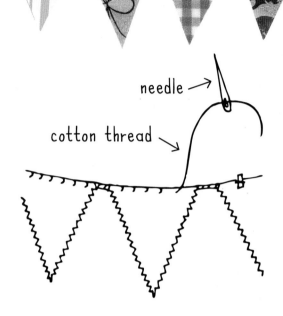

needle →

cotton thread ↘

x9

4. Repeat this process until all the diamonds are in place, leaving a little space between each. Make sure you have enough cord at each end to tie up your bunting when it's finished.

5. Thread a needle with a single cotton thread (see pages 3 to 4) and, using the overcast stitch (see pages 6 to 7), attach your diamonds to the cord. Push the needle into the cord and loop over the top.

Take the clothespins off before you start sewing each diamond.

6. Knot the thread (see pages 4 and 8) and repeat this process till all your diamonds are secured to the cord.

TIE YOUR BUNTING TO
YOUR BEDROOM WINDOW,
TO A PORCH OUTSIDE,
OR AGAINST THE WALL.

TOP TIPS

* Your bunting doesn't have to be a diamond shape—try a series of rectangles or perhaps some long, drooping semicircles.
* For a party, you might be able to find material that fits your theme, such as fairies, pirates, or ponies.

Come to the party! Join in the fun!

Fluttering hands wave everyone in.

To run and to play; to dance and to sing!

OWL CANVAS

Hoot! Hoot! Create your own little feathery friend to watch over you with this adorable fabric owl canvas. Hoot! Cute!

Time

2 to 3 hours plus 2 hours of drying time

Level of difficulty

Some delicate cutting required.

You will need

* Some scraps of 4 different patterned fabrics
* 1 piece of plain-colored fabric no smaller than 16 in. × 16 in. (for the background)
* Butcher or tracing paper (to copy your pattern)
* 1 plain canvas, 10 in. × 8 in.
* 16 to 20 thumbtacks with flat tops
* 2 plastic eyes
* Fabric glue
* Craft glue
* Popsicle stick or paintbrush
* Paper or plastic plate
* Scissors
* Ruler

40

HOW TO MAKE YOUR OWL CANVAS

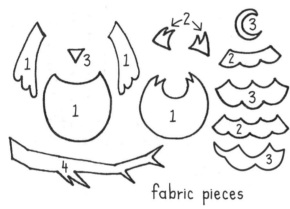

fabric pieces

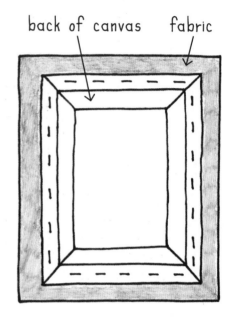

back of canvas   fabric

1. Copy the pattern on page 47 and cut out the shapes. You may need to enlarge the pattern on a copier so the owl design fills your canvas. Pin the pattern pieces onto your fabric and cut out your fabric pieces. Use the same fabric for the same number—for instance, all number 1 shapes in brown, all number 2 shapes in orange, and so on. Put aside for now.

2. Lay your canvas facedown in the center of the large piece of plain fabric.

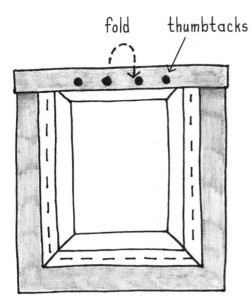

fold   thumbtacks

thumbtacks   fold

3. Pull the top of the material down over the canvas against the wooden frame and press four thumbtacks into the wood along its length to keep the fabric in place, leaving about 1¼ inches at each end for folding the corners in later.

4. Repeat step 3 on the opposite end of your canvas, gently pulling the canvas across so it is taut.

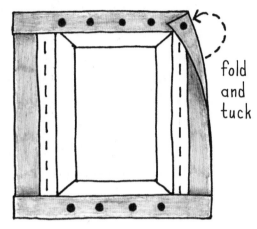

fold
and
tuck

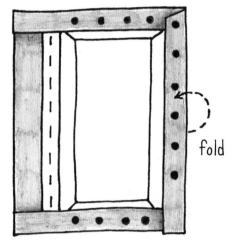

fold

5. Tuck one corner of the canvas in as if you were folding a present and secure it with a thumbtack.

6. Pull the material over the longer side of your canvas, starting from your tucked-in corner. Secure the fabric along the length of the wood with some thumbtacks.

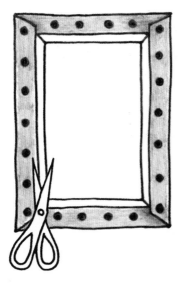

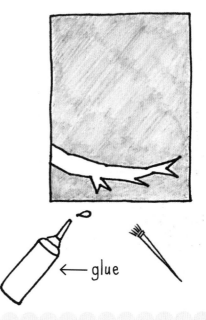

← glue

7. Tuck in the corner at the end of this side of the canvas and continue pinning and tucking till all sides are secured, then trim any excess backing material.

8. Lay your fabric pieces out on the front of your covered canvas before you glue them down to make sure you are happy with their position. Starting with the branch (numbered 4), apply some fabric glue (or Elmer's Glue, if you prefer) to the back of the cut shape using a paintbrush or Popsicle stick, making sure you paint right out to the edges. Then gently press the shape into position.

← glue

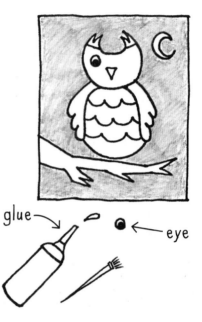

glue →

← eye

9. Repeat step 8 with the other pieces until all are in place: the head and the large body piece (numbered 1), then the feathers (numbered 2 and 3) and the wings (numbered 1). Glue the rest of the pieces in any order, then let stand to dry for 1 hour.

10. Place a small dab of craft glue onto the backs of the plastic eyes and gently press them onto the owl's face. Leave to dry for 10 minutes.

Pattern Pieces

HOOT! HOOT! YOUR LITTLE OWL IS READY TO HANG ON YOUR WALL AND WATCH OVER YOU WHILE YOU SLEEP.

TOP TIP

* You can make any design for this canvas—it doesn't have to be an owl. Try an elephant, flower, or fish. It's always best to cut out your pieces and lay them on your canvas first, before you glue them into place.

Midnight eyes watch over us, as we dream in our little beds.

A call from the Wild in the pearl moonlight,
Hoooooot!

~FROG PURSE~

Rrrribit! Grrrribit!
Here's one little frog
who will not hop away.
Lucky, because he'll be
a good spot for your
pocket money.

Time
2 hours plus 1 hour of drying
time for the glued fabric

Level of difficulty
A fairly difficult stitch is
used for the Frog.

You will need
* 1 piece each of green felt,
  yellow felt, and black felt
* Some dark brown
  embroidery thread
* Sewing needle with a large eye
* Fabric glue
* Paintbrush or Popsicle stick
* Paper or plastic plate
* Small piece of colorful patterned
  fabric
* Butcher or tracing paper
  (to copy your pattern)
* Ruler
* Small piece of Velcro about
  1 in. × 1 in. with adhesive
  backing
* Some clothespins
* Scissors

HOW TO MAKE YOUR FROG PURSE

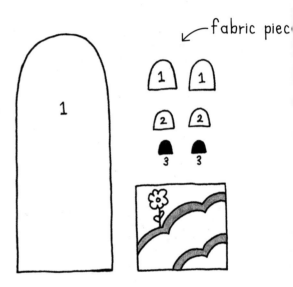

fabric piece

1

1   1

2   2

3   3

1. Make a copy of the pattern on page 57. Pin this onto your felt and cut out your shapes—green felt for pieces numbered 1, yellow felt for pieces numbered 2, and black felt for pieces numbered 3. Your square piece of patterned fabric should be even on all sides and the same width as the square end of the large piece of felt.

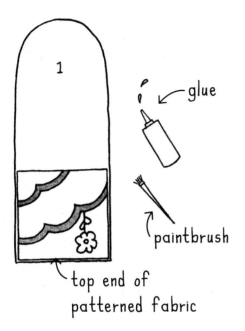

1

glue

paintbrush

top end of
patterned fabric

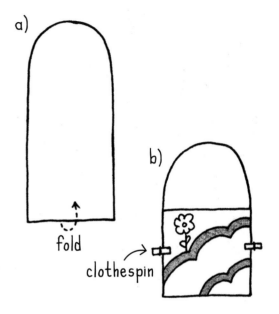

a)

b)

fold

clothespin

2. Paint some fabric glue onto the back of
your square of patterned fabric and press
it down onto the base of the long piece
of green felt. If your piece of fabric has a
picture or a pattern right side up, make
sure it is sitting so that the top of the
picture or pattern is right at the edge of
the felt (as shown above). Allow 1 hour to
dry.

3. Place the long green piece facedown
so that the fabric square cannot be seen,
then fold the fabric square back onto
the felt and secure with some clothespins
on either side.

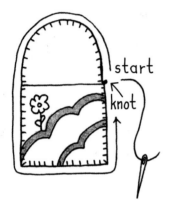

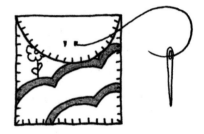

4. Thread a needle with a single embroidery thread and, beginning at the bottom right-hand corner, blanket-stitch all the way around the purse. Make sure you sew right over the arched curve at the top of the purse and along the fold at the bottom. Knot the thread when you reach the end. (See the "Stitches" section, pages 3 to 6, for all skills needed here.)

5. Fold the arched end of the purse down over the patterned fabric and, using the same embroidery thread, make two small stitches for the nose of the frog, then knot. (Be careful not to sew right through the purse— just sew through the arched end.)

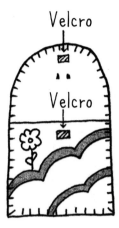

Velcro

Velcro

glue

glue

finished eye

6. Fold the arched end back and press one piece of the adhesive Velcro onto the back of the frog's face. Then line up your other piece of Velcro and place this on the patterned fabric.

7. Using a paintbrush or Popsicle stick, apply fabric glue to the smaller eye arches and stick these to the large eye arches.

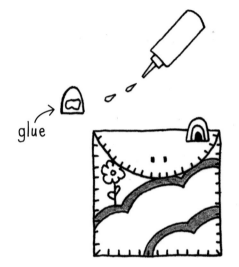

glue

8. Paint some glue onto the bottom half of your eye arches and press them firmly into place on the top half of the frog's face.

9. Allow to dry (about 20 minutes).

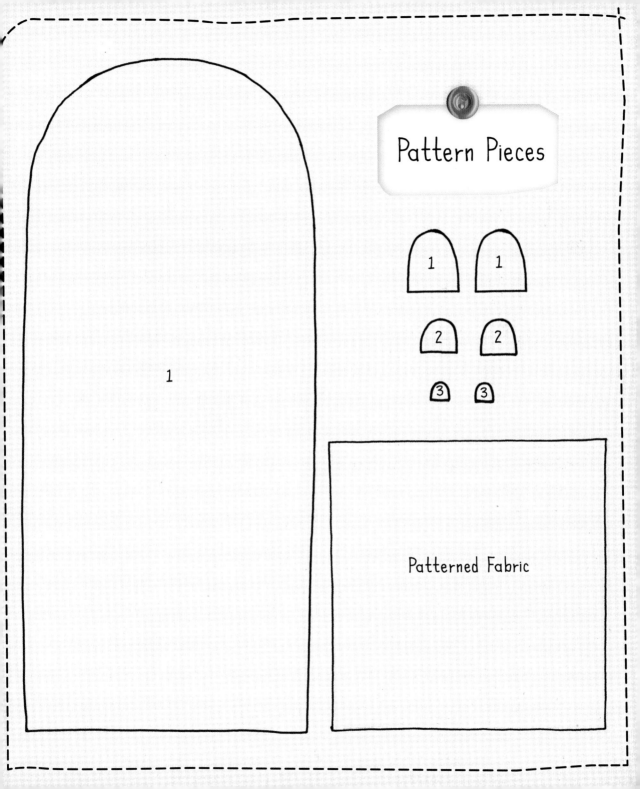

Pattern Pieces

1

1 1

2 2

3 3

Patterned Fabric

RRRRIBIT! YOUR FROG IS NOW READY TO USE.

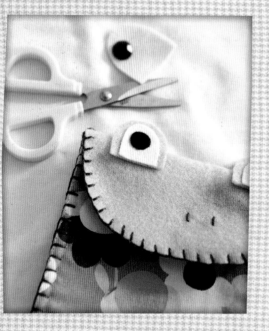

TOP TIP

* You can have the basic shape (the big, long, green pattern) in a different color and create any other animal you like by adding ears and whiskers—a cat or dog? Or let your imagination run wild and create something crazy!

Rrrrrrrribbit!
Grrrrrrribbit!
Hop!
Hop! Hop!

LAVENDER COCOONS

These fragrant and pretty creations have been made since Elizabethan times, when ladies would sit together, weaving them to scent their wardrobes and cupboards. These lavender cocoons are a bit more colorful than the Elizabethan ones, though, so hang them on a door handle, by a window, or any other place where they can be seen.

Time
About 30 minutes per cocoon

Level of difficulty

You will need
* Some long pieces of ribbon or strips of fabric, no wider than ½ in. and about 1 yd. long
* Scissors
* Some long stems of fresh lavender (You will need about 5 to 7 per cocoon.)

HOW TO MAKE YOUR LAVENDER COCOON

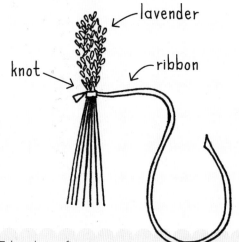

lavender

knot

ribbon

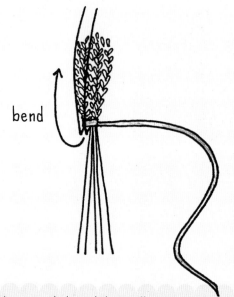

bend

1. Take about five to seven lavender stems (make it an odd number) and tie them together at the base of the flowers with one end of your fabric or ribbon. Make sure you knot the end well.

2. Very gently bend the stalks (the stick part of the lavender) back toward the tips of the flowers.

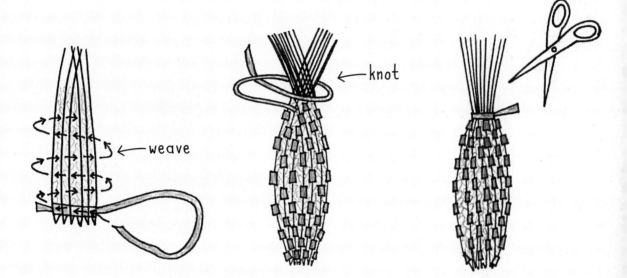

weave

← knot

3. Once you have bent them all back, find the loose end of the ribbon at the base where the knot is, and weave it through the stems by threading it under one stem then passing it over the top of the next stem and so on.

4. Once you have reached the top of the flowers, knot the ribbon by looping it around the top of the stems and tucking it under the loop.

5. Trim the stems and the leftover ribbon, leaving about 1 inch at the end.

AND THERE YOU HAVE IT—
A LITTLE SCENTED COCOON.
THEY LOOK GORGEOUS IN A
LITTLE BUNCH TIED TOGETHER
WITH SOME RIBBON.

TOP TIPS

* For a nicer finish, try to keep the ribbon or fabric flat and untwisted as you weave.
* Try gluing some beads or sequins to your cocoons and then hanging them on the Christmas tree as fancy decorations.

Huddled in,
tucked up tight,
purple pods in
snug cocoons.

Open up your
darling buds,

And scent
the skies
with calming
blooms.

PINCUSHIONS

Try this cute little creation—a lovely gift for other crafty people. Have fun with different patterned fabric for the top and bottom, and go crazy with quirky buttons to give your pincushions a unique look.

Time
About 1 hour per cushion

Level of difficulty

You will need
* Needle
* Cotton thread
* Cotton wool or Dacron filling
* 1 large button
* Ruler
* 2 pieces of fabric about 4 in. × 4 in. each
* Scissors

HOW TO MAKE YOUR
PINCUSHION

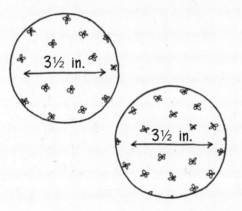

3½ in.

3½ in.

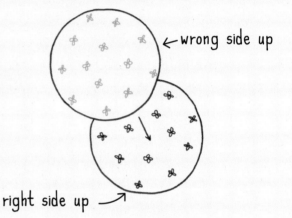

← wrong side up

right side up →

1. Cut two circles from your fabric, no less than 3½ inches wide. Do not worry if your circles are not completely round as long as they are a similar shape.

2. Place the two circles on top of each other with the pattern (or right side) facing inward. This means that you will not be able to see the brightest side of the material while you sew. Don't worry— you will eventually turn it inside out!

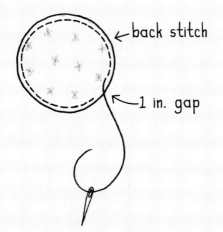

← back stitch

←—1 in. gap

a)

b)

filling

3. Thread a needle with a single cotton thread and, using the back stitch technique, sew the two pieces of material together. Remember to sew at least ¼ inch in from the edge for the seam allowance, and make sure you also finish about 1 inch before the end so you can turn your pincushion inside out. Knot the end of the cotton and cut the thread. (See the "Stitches" section, pages 3 to 8, for all skills needed here.)

4. Pull the pincushion through the opening you have created at the top until it is completely inside out (with the pattern now right side out) and stuff it with cotton wool filling until the pincushion is quite plump.

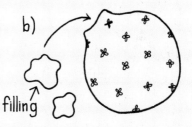

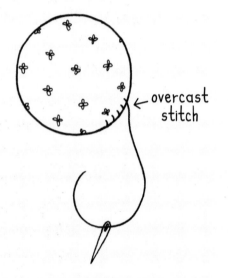

overcast ← stitch

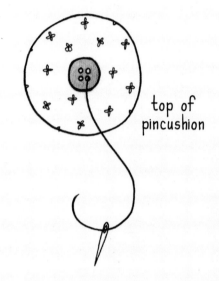

top of pincushion

5. Tuck in the edges of the material and sew up the opening using overcast stitch. Knot the end when you have sealed the hole.

6. Thread the needle again with a single cotton thread and push it through the center of the pincushion to the top of the other side, making sure that the needle comes out at the center again. Then thread the large button onto the needle.

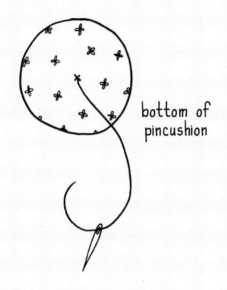

bottom of
pincushion

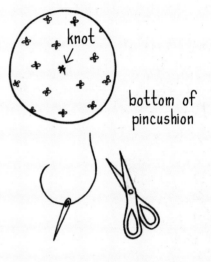

knot

bottom of
pincushion

7. Loop over and push the needle through another hole on the button back to the other side of the pincushion. Pull it firmly so that your pincushion pinches in at the center.

8. Repeat the above step about three times to secure the button firmly, then knot the thread at the base of your pincushion (on the opposite side from the button) and cut the thread.

YOUR CUTE LITTLE **PINCUSHION** IS NOW READY TO USE—A HOME FOR YOUR PINS!

TOP TIP

* You don't have to use circles for this project—you could try a heart shape, a star, or even a simple square. Just make sure your shape isn't too tricky for you to be able to sew and stuff it.

Pinwheels turning, turning, buttons spinning, colors swirling, shapes unfurling...

...watch them whirling. See the rainbows come to life!

LEAF MOBILE

A stylish and beautiful piece of art, sure to attract attention—it's like bringing nature into your home. And it's so simple to make!

Time
About 2 hours

Level of difficulty

You will need
* Sewing needle with a large eye
* Some scraps of fabric in different colors and patterns (no smaller than 4 in. × 4 in.). It's best to use heavier fabric that won't flop around too much.
* 3 lengths of string at least 1 yd. long
* A fairly straight stick or piece of driftwood at least 12 in. long
* Ruler
* Scissors

HOW TO MAKE YOUR LEAF MOBILE

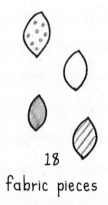

18
fabric pieces

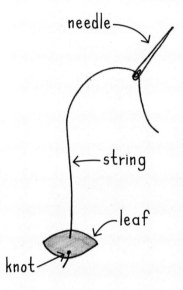

needle

string

leaf

knot

1. Cut eighteen pieces of fabric into a leaf shape roughly 3¼ inches long and 2 inches wide.

2. Thread the needle with your string, using a single thread (see pages 3 to 4), and knot. Push the needle through the middle of the bottom curve of one fabric leaf, pulling the leaf down to the knot. Then push the needle through the middle of the top curve of your fabric leaf, pulling through until you have one large stitch across the leaf.

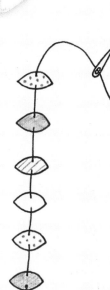

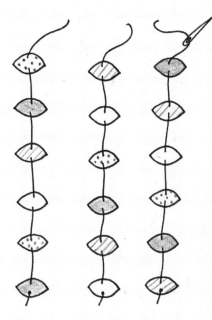

3. Repeat step 2 with six more leaves, making sure there is some space between each (about 2 inches). Leave at least 16 inches at the top of the string clear of leaves so you can tie it to the stick and still have string left for hanging your mobile.

4. Repeat with the other two lengths of string.

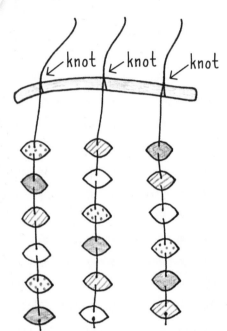

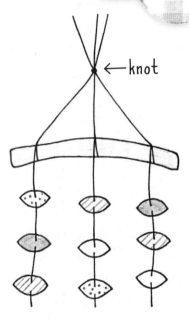

5. Tie the leaf strings onto your stick or driftwood about 2 inches above the last leaf and knot each string twice at the top.

6. Pull the three strings together at the top so they form a triangle and knot them together by making a loop and pushing the string through.

7. About 1½ inches above this knot, make another, similar knot and then trim the extra string off at the top.

NOW HANG YOUR STYLISH LEAF MOBILE IN A PLACE WHERE EVERYONE CAN ADMIRE IT.

TOP TIPS

* For a beautiful jingly sound, thread some small bells after each leaf.
* Add a little stitch to some leaves for decoration.
* If leaves aren't your thing, try a different shape—ovals or stars, or perhaps some pretty flower shapes.

An autumn leaf in full flight,

Fluttering in a light-speckled sky.

Catching the wind and sailing by . . .

FESTIVE WREATH

Not just for Christmastime, this stunning wreath looks extremely stylish when hung on a bare wall. And it's one of the simplest projects in this book!

Time
About 1½ hours

Level of difficulty
● Very easy

You will need
* Some fabric—different colors and patterns
* Scissors
* An embroidery hoop

HOW TO MAKE YOUR FESTIVE WREATH

fabric strips

1. Cut some strips of fabric about 1 inch wide and 8 inches long. You will need quite a few strips, so allow at least an hour for cutting! You can always cut more if you find you don't have enough halfway through your project.

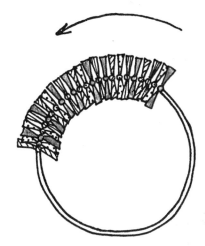

2. Your embroidery ring is actually made up of *two* rings, but you only need one (why not save the other for another Festive Wreath!). Using one of the rings, tie a strip of fabric around the ring, making a double knot.

3. Repeat this process until you have made your way all around the ring. Make sure your strips of fabric are as close together as you can manage to create a thick and bushy wreath.

WHEN YOU HAVE FINISHED YOUR WREATH, HANG IT ON A HOOK IN THE WALL OR ON A DOOR. HOW GOOD DOES IT LOOK?!

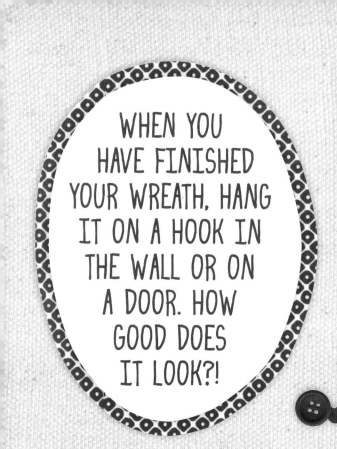

TOP TIP

* Try just two colors for a simple wreath, or go crazy with every color in the rainbow!

A symbol of peace, for the festive season. A sign of goodwill, a circle of joy. Gladness to all, for a special occasion — to all living things, every girl, every boy. * A symbol of peace, for

FUNKY PICTURE HANGER

With this hanger you can change or rearrange your artwork display as often as you like. Or you can even clip up some cherished photos of family and friends.

Time
About 1½ hours

Level of difficulty

You will need
* Craft glue
* Fabric glue
* Popsicle stick or paintbrush
* Paper or plastic plate
* A length of cotton cord or thick string no less than 1 yd. long
* Some scraps of felt in different colors
* Some scraps of material in different colors and patterns
* Scissors
* Ruler
* 5 small clothespins about 2 in. long (from most craft stores)

HOW TO MAKE YOUR FUNKY PICTURE HANGER

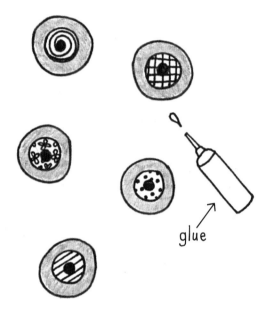

glue

fabric and felt circles

1. Cut out some circles from your felt and fabric with three different diameters—2 inches, 1¼ inches, and 1 inch. Cut about five of each. Don't worry if your circles aren't perfect—an uneven circle makes your picture hanger even more interesting.

2. Using your Popsicle stick or paintbrush, scrape a little fabric glue onto the backs of your smaller circles, and one at a time, press these gently onto the larger circles. Make sure the smallest circles are on the top. Put to the side and allow to dry (about 20 minutes).

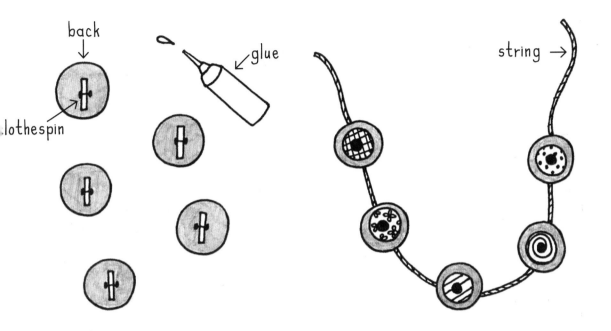

back

glue

string →

lothespin

3. Lay each dry circle onto a flat surface, pattern side facing down. Apply a thin layer of craft glue to one flat side of your clothespins and gently press the glued side onto the circles. Allow to dry for another 10 minutes.

4. Pin the circles onto the string with a little space between each.

ALL YOU HAVE TO
DO NOW IS TIE
THE STRING AT
EITHER END ACROSS
A WALL, FIREPLACE,
OR EVEN A WINDOW
AND CLIP UP YOUR
TREASURED ARTWORK
AND PHOTOS.

TOP TIPS

* Circles are very simple, but for something different and a bit more challenging, try flowers, leaves, stars, bird shapes— anything you like!
* Glue some buttons to the circles for a quirky look.

Capturing memories in a perfect picture frame.

Faces and favorites, again and again.

The funny, the crazy, the moments past.

Each happy treasure, from the first to the last!

LOVE

PAPER LANTERNS

Stunning lanterns as a centerpiece for your dining table or outside at dusk on a warm, balmy night. Make each evening special with these simple and twinkly creations.

Caution: Always ask an adult to help when placing lit tea-light candles inside the lanterns, and never leave lit lanterns unattended.

Time

About 30 to 40 minutes for each lantern

Level of difficulty

The cutting and pasting can be a bit tricky.

You will need

* Some letter-sized (8½ in. x 11 in.) sheets of transparent-style paper (I have used different colored cobweb paper for my lanterns, which is available at most craft and fabric stores.)
* Glue stick or Elmer's Glue
* A few clothespins (any size)
* A hole punch (available from craft stores—get one that is used like a pair of pliers and not the square kind)
* Some letter-sized sheets of card stock
* Scissors

HOW TO MAKE YOUR
PAPER LANTERN

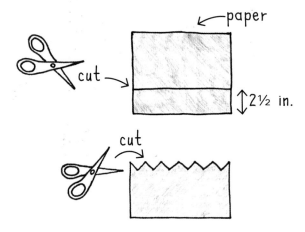

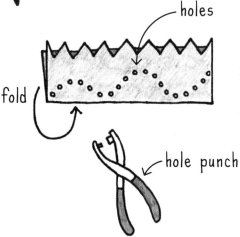

1. Cut about 2½ inches off one edge of your letter-sized sheets of transparent paper, lengthways, and cut a crown-type pattern on the other edge.

2. Fold the paper in half so that the crown edge meets the straight edge of the paper. Using your hole punch, make some holes in a swirly or wavelike pattern along the folded edge of your paper.

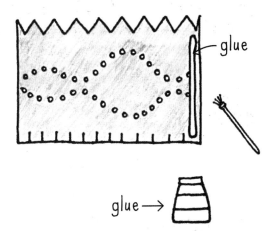

3. Unfold the paper and smooth out the crease in the middle, then snip ("snip" means a little cut) all the way along the bottom edge of the paper about ½ inch into the edge and ½ inch apart.

4. Apply a small amount of glue on the inside of one end of your paper, just along the edge (about ½ inch in).

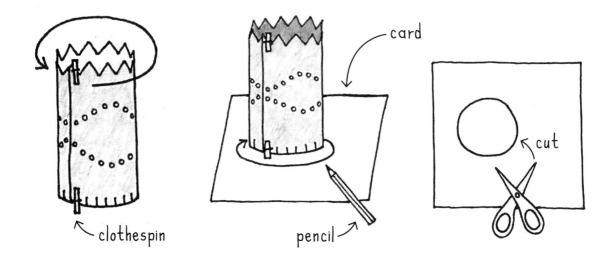

clothespin

card

pencil

cut

5. Curve the sides of the paper around and press them together at the glued edge. Clip at the top and bottom to secure the sides.

6. While you wait for the glue to dry, place your clipped lantern on top of your letter-sized card stock and lightly trace a circle around the lantern (this will be your base). Then cut out the circle and place it to the side.

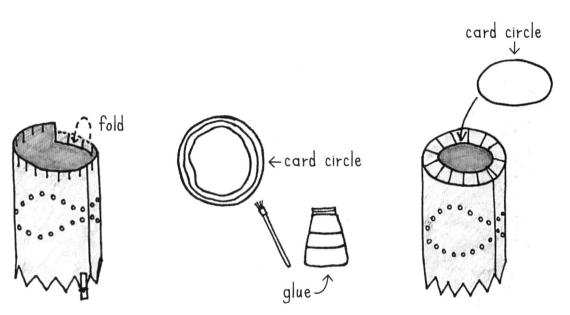

fold

←card circle

card circle
↓

glue ⤴

7. When the glue on your lantern is dry (about 20 minutes), remove the bottom clothespin and begin to fold in the snipped edge at the base. Make sure you fold toward the center of your lantern.

8. Apply some glue to the outer edge of your circle.

9. Place the card circle onto the pressed-down snips and press it onto the glued surface by placing your hand up through the top of the lantern.

NOW WAIT FOR THE BASE TO DRY (ANOTHER 20 MINUTES) BEFORE PLACING A LIT TEA LIGHT IN THE CENTER OF YOUR LANTERN, WITH THE HELP OF AN ADULT.

TOP TIP

* Make a few lanterns in different colored paper and place them in the center of a table. Watch the candle shine through the little holes you made with your hole punch—they look like twinkling stars!

I saw a light and followed it to the foot of a blossom tree.

And looking up, I smiled with joy,

For every bough glimmering bright with lanterns did I see!

PONY FRIEND

This **adorable** little friend is more than happy to have you snuggled against him, dreaming of wildflowers and open plains.

Time

About 2 hours

Level of difficulty

It uses that back stitch, which you may need to practice!

You will need

* Some fabric of your choice (anything!), large enough to cut 2 pieces of the pattern on page 109
* Butcher or tracing paper (to copy your pattern)
* A small roll of thick wool (any color)
* 1 needle with a large eye
* 1 needle with a smaller eye
* 1 reel of cotton to match your fabric
* 1 small bag of cotton filling or a wad of cotton wool
* Scissors
* Ruler

HOW TO MAKE YOUR PONY FRIEND

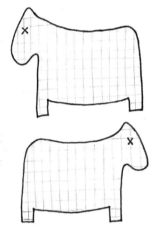

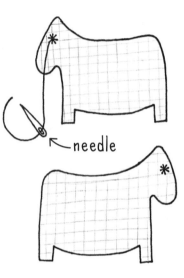

needle

1. Make a copy of the pattern supplied on page 109 (enlarged on a copier, if you like) and cut out two horse shapes. Remember to flip the pattern for your second piece so the patterned side of the fabric will be facing out each side of the horse, then make a little "X" mark with a pencil on the patterned side of each piece for where the eye will be sewn.

2. Now thread your large needle with the wool, using a single thread (see pages 3 to 4), and sew a star or a round circle or even a button where the "X" is.

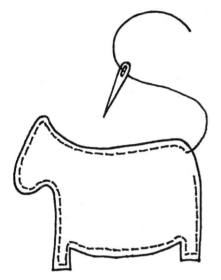

pull
through

3. Place your two pieces together with the patterned sides of the fabric facing inward. Thread the small needle with your cotton and stitch around about ¼ inch from the edge of the horse using a back stitch. Make sure you leave an unstitched section at the horse's bottom to stuff it (hee hee!). Then knot your thread at the end. (See the "Stitches" section, pages 3 to 8, for all skills needed here.)

4. Turn your horse inside out by pulling the fabric through the gap in the horse's bottom. The horse will now be right side out with the pattern showing.

stuffing

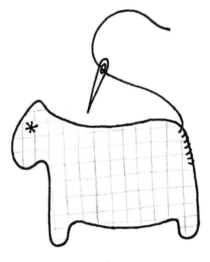

5. Now stuff your horse with the cotton wool until he is quite plump.

6. Thread the small needle with the cotton, using a double thread. Using the overcast stitch (see pages 6 to 7), seal up the bottom of your horse and knot the end of the thread.

7. Next, you will make the horse's mane. Neigh! Cut twenty-one pieces of your wool, each 8 inches long. Using one strand at a time, thread the wool through the large needle (don't make a knot at the end) and push it through the material at the top of the horse's head till the thread is even on both sides, then pull the needle off the thread. Continue along the top of your horse's head and down its neck in bunches of three strands with a little space in between.

8. Once all the threads are in place, take both sides of one bunch at a time and make a double knot in the middle of each to stop the threads from pulling out.

9. Now for the horse's tail. Swish! Cut nine pieces of the wool, each 8 inches long, and tie them together in a knot at the top.

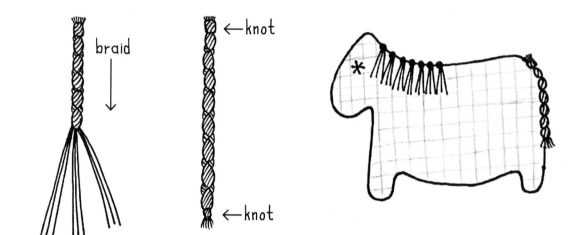

10. Now divide the wool into three lots of three strands and braid it. Leave enough room at the end to make another knot.

11. Thread the small needle with the cotton, using a double thread (see pages 3 to 4) and knot at the end. Then sew your horse's tail to his bottom, knot the end of your thread, and cut the needle free!

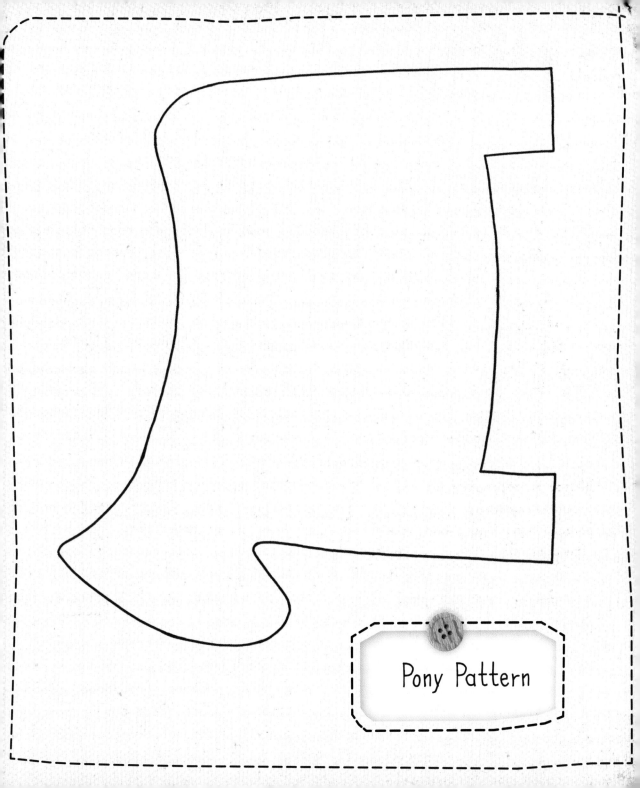

Pony Pattern

AND THERE!
YOU NOW HAVE A
SPECIAL NEW FRIEND!
AND YOUR LITTLE
HORSE IS VERY GOOD
AT KEEPING SECRETS
SHOULD YOU WISH
TO TELL HIM YOURS.

TOP TIPS

* If you are not very confident
  with embroidering the eye,
  try gluing or sewing a button or
  funny plastic googly eye
  to your horse.
* You don't have to braid your
  horse's tail. You can leave it
  straggly and flowing. Just make
  sure you have knotted your
  strands at the top—this will
  make it easier to fasten the tail
  to the back of your horse.

Free! He gallops, the wind in his mane. Crossing meadows and rocky terrain. A special friend forever.

CAT BOOKMARK

Time

About 30 minutes plus 1 hour of drying time for the glue

Level of difficulty

You will need

* 1 piece each of light brown and dark brown felt
* A small piece of colorful patterned fabric, about 4 in. wide and 8 in. long
* 1 small strip of fabric or ribbon and 1 small button, sequin, or bead (for the cat's collar and bell)
* Butcher or tracing paper (to copy your pattern)
* Dark brown or black embroidery thread
* A sewing needle with a large eye
* Fabric glue
* Paintbrush or Popsicle stick
* Paper or plastic plate
* Ruler
* Scissors

Meow! Meow!

Cats may not read (not that we know of, anyway), but I have seen plenty of cats curled up in sunny spots in bookshops, which proves they are fond of being around books. Create your own little book-loving feline to help you remember which page you are up to in your latest favorite story.

HOW TO MAKE
YOUR CAT
BOOKMARK

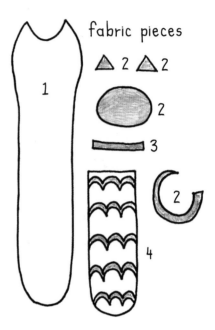

fabric pieces

1. **Make a copy of the pattern on page 117 and cut out your felt shapes. Use the light brown felt for the piece numbered 1, the dark brown felt for the pieces numbered 2, and the small strip of fabric or ribbon for the piece numbered 3. The piece labeled 4 is for the patterned fabric.**

a)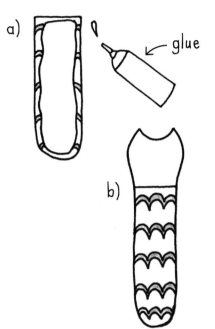

glue

b)

needle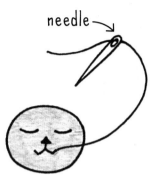

2. a) Using your Popsicle stick or paintbrush, apply some fabric glue onto the back of your small piece of colorful patterned fabric.
b) Press the fabric down onto the bottom section of the long piece of cat-shaped brown felt. Allow 1 hour to dry.

3. While your felt piece is drying, thread a large needle with a single dark brown or black embroidery thread (see pages 3 to 4) and sew a little cat face onto the oval piece of brown felt.

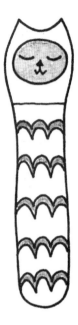

4. Apply some fabric glue to the back of the cat face and press it down onto the rounded cat head of your long piece of felt.

5. Paint some glue onto the tail, ears, and collar and press them into place. Add a small drop of glue onto the back of the little button, sequin, or bead and place this on the collar. Allow to dry for 1 hour.

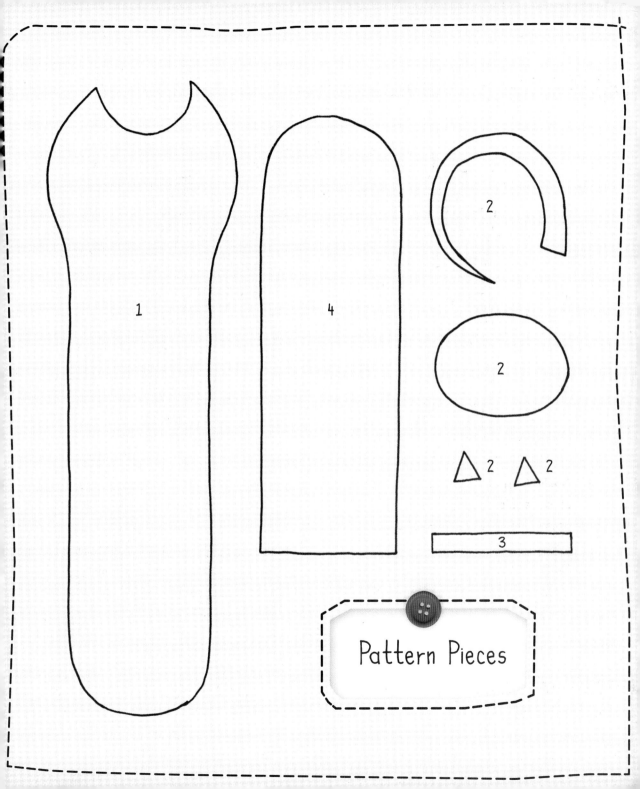

1

4

2

2

2   2

3

Pattern Pieces

TA-DA! MEOW! WHAT A CUTE LITTLE READING FRIEND!

TOP TIP

* If sewing the cat's face is a little tricky, try gluing some beads for the nose and eyes and some strips of dark felt for the whiskers. Or you could draw the face using a fine black permanent marker.

Little Cat naps atop a shelf of books...

WILD THING PUPPET

Time
1½ hours

Level of difficulty
Blanket stitch is required.

You will need
* 2 pieces of felt in one color (say, green) and 1 piece of felt in another color (say, red). The felt comes in ready-cut pieces from craft and fabric stores.
* 1 piece of any material you have spare (patterned is fun)
* Butcher or tracing paper (to copy your pattern)
* About 1 yd. of thick wool
* Embroidery thread (any color)
* Needle with a large eye
* Fabric glue
* Small paintbrush or Popsicle stick
* Paper or plastic plate
* Scissors
* Ruler

Hideously cute, this little monster puppet is more fun than scary. But feel free to dress him up with other bits and pieces to make him more terrible—googly eyes or a blotch of fabric blood will work a treat!

HOW TO MAKE YOUR WILD THING

fabric pieces

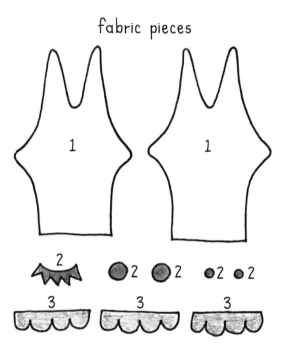

1. Make a copy of the pattern on page 125 and cut out your felt shapes. The two larger shapes should be bigger than your hand (so your hand can fit into the puppet). Pieces numbered 1 are for the green felt, those numbered 2 are for the red felt, and those numbered 3 are for any other material.

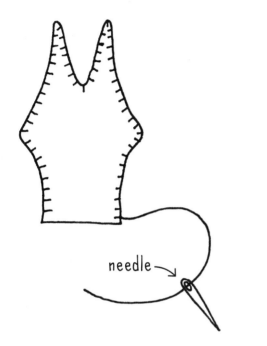

needle

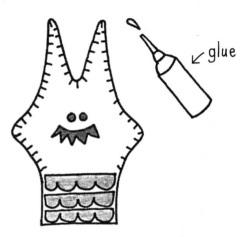

glue

2. Place the two largest green pieces of felt together and sew them around the edge using a blanket stitch (see pages 5 to 6). Don't worry if the stitch causes the ears to bunch up a bit at the very tip—you will be able to disguise this with your wool later on. Knot the thread and cut.

3. With your paintbrush or Popsicle stick, apply some fabric glue onto the backs of all the other pieces except the larger number 2 felt circles. Press them into place as shown in the drawing above. Wait 30 minutes for the glue to dry.

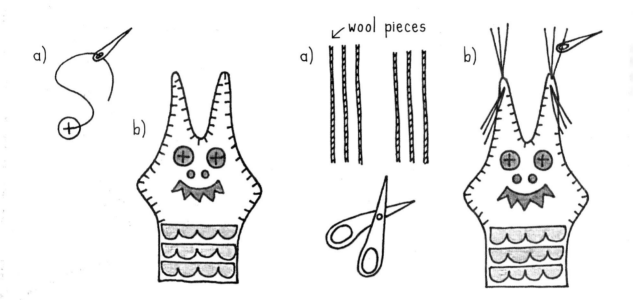

wool pieces

a)

b)

a)

b)

4. a) Now thread your large needle with the wool, using a single thread (see pages 3 to 4), and sew a cross over each eye piece (the larger pair of number 2 felt circles). Knot and cut the thread.
b) Now glue the eyes to your puppet.

5. a) Cut six 5-inch lengths of your wool.
b) Using one strand at a time, with no knot at the end, thread the wool through the large needle and push it through the material at the top of the Monster's ears till the thread is halfway through (three threads per ear). Now tie up the threads with a double knot at the top of each ear.

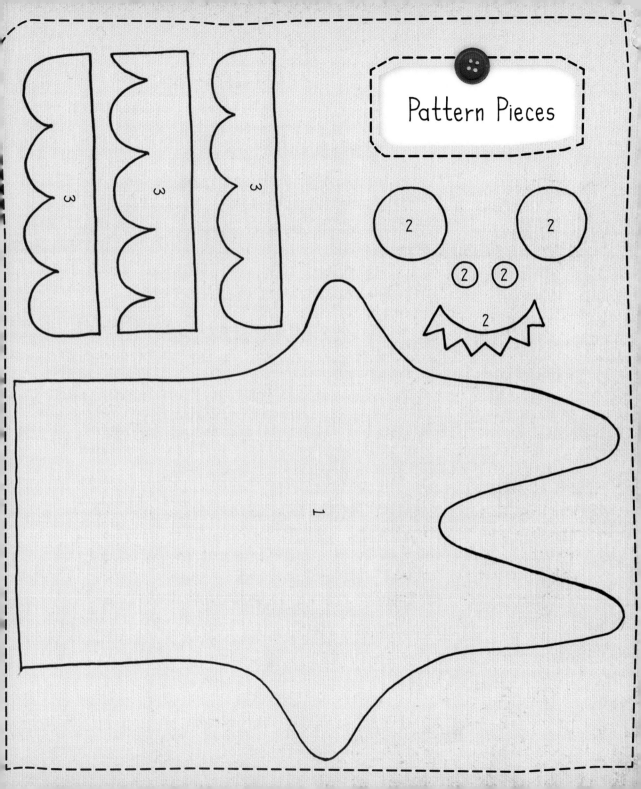

Pattern Pieces

3 3 3

2 2

2 2

2

1

ROOOOAAAARRRR!!!!
A TERRIFIC BUT NOT
TOO TERRIFYING
LITTLE BEAST TO
PLAY WITH.

TOP TIPS

* Make sure you push your middle and index fingers up into the Monster's ears to make them wiggle.
* You don't have to use green and red felt—you can go crazy with colors. But try to stick to felt, as it will not fray like other fabrics.

LITTLE MAT

You can make this mat as large or as small as you like. A little mat is perfect for a teapot to sit on, and a larger mat could even become a rug if you have a few weeks to spare! Look out—this project has the potential to become endless! These mats are perfect for pets, too.

Time

30 minutes to days or even weeks!

Level of difficulty

The braiding can get long and difficult to control!

You will need

* Some strips of fabric about 1 yd. long and anything up to 4 in. wide
* Needle with a small eye
* White cotton thread
* Scissors

HOW TO MAKE YOUR LITTLE MAT

1. ←knot
2. braid

1. Cut three strips of fabric. (Don't worry if they are not perfectly straight.) Knot them together at one end.

2. Next, braid your fabric strips, leaving enough room at the end to knot them together.

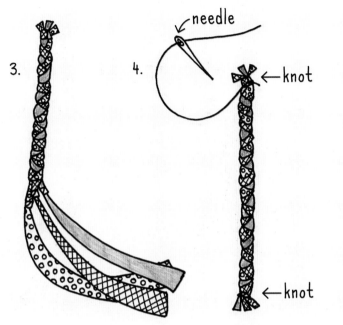

3. At this point you can add to the length of your braid by tying on three more strips of fabric to the ends of your first three strips.

4. When you think your braid is long enough, knot the end. Then thread a needle using a single thread and knot the end. Push the needle through one end of the braid, pulling it through till the knot in the thread catches.

5. Beginning at one end of the braid, curl it around the knot, sewing the edges of the braid to the knot as you go, using the overcast stitch (see pages 6 to 7). Continue until you have completely coiled the braid and then sew the end knot to the edge of your rug securely. Knot the cotton thread and cut the needle free.

THIS IS ANOTHER ONE OF THOSE CRAFT ACTIVITIES THAT IS GREAT TO DO WITH A FRIEND AND COULD KEEP YOU BOTH OCCUPIED FOR HOURS.

TOP TIPS

* Try using material in just two colors—maybe red and white—for a classic and sophisticated rug.
* To get an idea of how long your mat will be before you do your last knot, secure the end with a clothespin and then coil the braid loosely in a spiral, holding it in place with one hand and coiling with the other. If it's not as big as you need, tie more strips onto your braid.

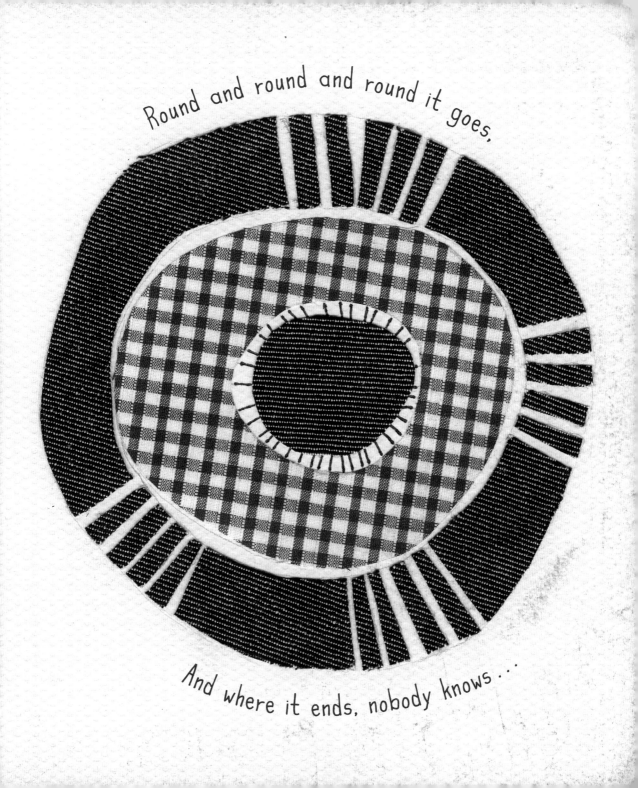

FABRIC AND PAPER CREDITS

EVERY EFFORT has been made to trace and acknowledge the fabric and paper designers and manufacturers whose materials are shown in this book. The publisher would be pleased to hear from any copyright holders who have not been acknowledged.

Lace-Pressed Brooch
Fabrics: *Spotlight* (flowers and vintage blue lace)
Paper: *Cristina Re Designs* (spotted)

Paper Beads
Paper: Japanese

Button Rings
Fabrics: *Spotlight* (polka-dot fabric); vintage (floral)

Bunting
Fabrics: *Spotlight* (gingham and skull and crossbones); vintage linen
Paper: *Cristina Re Designs* and Japanese

Owl Canvas
Fabrics: *Patchwork on Central Park* (floral); *Est Australia* (gingham linen); vintage linen (tartan and spotted)

Frog Purse
Fabrics: *Spotlight* (background green); *Patchwork on Central Park* (floral square and border)

Lavender Cocoons
Fabrics: Vintage (gingham border); *Patchwork on Central Park* (pots and Cocoon fabrics); *Flashback Fabric* (Cocoons)

Pincushions
Fabrics: Vintage (border and linen); *Patchwork on Central Park* (Pincushion fabrics)

Leaf Mobile
Fabrics: *Est Australia* (gingham linen clouds and plain linen border); various upholstery for Leaf Mobile.
Paper: *Basic Grey Designs*

Festive Wreath
Fabrics: *Spotlight* and vintage
(Wreath material)
Paper: Japanese

Funky Picture Hanger
Fabrics: *Patchwork on Central Park*
(background fabric); *Spotlight* and *Patchwork
on Central Park* (Picture Hanger dots)

Paper Lanterns
Fabrics: Vintage.
Paper: *Cristina Re Designs*

Pony Friend
Fabrics: *Flashback Fabric* (vintage border);
Patchwork on Central Park (Pony); various
upholstery and *Flashback Fabric* (trees
in collage)

Cat Bookmark
Fabrics: *Spotlight* (floral Cat body
and background)
Paper: *Cristina Re Designs* (background)

Wild Thing Puppet
Fabrics: *Spotlight* (Puppet felt and fabric)
Paper: Japanese

Little Mat
Fabrics: *Spotlight* (background); *Flashback
Fabric* and *Spotlight* (Mat fabrics)

SUPPLIER DETAILS

Michaels
www.michaels.com

Jo-Ann Fabrics & Craft Stores
www.joann.com

All Craft Supplies
www.allcraftsupplies.com

ABOUT THE
AUTHOR

KATIE EVANS is an editor in Books for Children and Young Adults at Penguin Books in Melbourne, Australia. Crafting is a big part of her family life, and she shares this passion (along with an out-of-control collection of vintage fabrics) with her mum and two kids. After dropping out of a BA in fine art many years ago, she traveled the world with a children's theater company, hosted parties for kids, and worked in too many restaurants as a waitress before coming back to the thing she loves most—creating beautiful things for herself and others. Katie feels it's important to encourage children to engage in a creative activity—especially with their friends—that promotes the sharing of ideas and builds on a host of other invaluable skills.

Katie lives in inner Melbourne with her two crafty children, two equally crafty cats, and a clever, craft-tolerant husband.

For more info, craft tips, and projects, visit **busythings.blogspot.com**

Acknowledgments

I would like to thank the following people in the making of this book: my parents, who have encouraged me to be creative and supported me in all my artistic endeavors; my husband and best friend, Dan, for his patience; my publisher, Laura Harris, for her vision, experience, and generosity; my editor, Heather Curdie, for her amazing management skills, attention to detail, and invaluable guidance; and the very talented Elissa Webb, whose superb design has taken this book to another level.